DINOSAURS

THE FASTEST
THE FIERCEST
THE MOST AMAZING

Written by Elizabeth MacLeod
Illustrated by Gordon Sauvé

Consultant: Dr. Philip J. Currie, Head, Dinosaur Research,
Royal Tyrrell Museum of Palaeontology

PUFFIN BOOKS

This is Earth 220 million years ago, when dinosaurs first lived. There are no grasses, just lots of ferns, some bushes, and a few giant pine trees. The weather is warm and wet. There are lots of animals that look like today's crocodiles, turtles, and lizards, but you have to look hard to see many spiders or furry animals.

In this book, you'll meet some of the most amazing dinosaurs ever. They are all different, but they share some things that make them dinosaurs. They all lived 65 to 220 million years ago. They lived on land — not underwater or in the air. And their legs were right under their bodies. That's different from a lizard's legs, which stick out at its sides.

So that you can see how really incredible these dinosaurs were, some of them have been paired up. That doesn't always mean they lived together or at the same time. To find out when they lived and how big they were compared to one another, turn to the chart at the back of the book.

Ready to meet some amazing dinosaurs?

THE FIRST DINOSAURS

Herrerasaurus is one of the oldest dinosaurs ever found. It wasn't a very fast runner, but it was a fierce hunter with a mouthful of sharp, jagged teeth. *Herrerasaurus* was about twice as long as you are when you lie down, but it probably wasn't even as tall as your waist.

Another of the first dinosaurs was *Coelophysis*. It was about the same size as *Herrerasaurus* and was a hunter, too. *Coelophysis* hunted in large packs, chasing down other dinosaurs and reptiles. They may have also hunted their own kind—skeletons of young *Coelophysis* have been found in the stomachs of older ones.

SMALLEST DINOSAUR

It's hard to imagine a dinosaur as tiny as a pigeon, but that's how big *Compsognathus* was. It probably looked a little like a bird, too, as it raced around on its back legs. It may even have had some feathers. Although *Compsognathus* was small, it was a good hunter. It used its sharp eyes and speed to help it catch lizards and insects.

LONGEST DINOSAUR

When *Seismosaurus* walked, the ground shook. It's the longest dinosaur found yet. This dinosaur was half as long as a football field and tall enough to peek into a fourth floor window. It weighed at least 44 tons (40 tonnes), or more than six elephants, but its head and teeth were only as big as a horse's. With teeth so small, *Seismosaurus* probably didn't bother to chew much. Instead, it ground up its food by swallowing stones that stayed in its stomach. *Seismosaurus* ate only plants and had to eat constantly to keep its huge body fed.

BIGGEST MEAT EATER

Tyrannosaurus was a huge dinosaur. Its jaws alone were longer than you are tall and it had 60 teeth, some as large as bananas. *Tyrannosaurus* attacked other dinosaurs by running into them with its jaws wide open. Then it used its tiny but strong front arms to hold on to its dinner. *Tyrannosaurus* had such a big stomach to fill that it wasn't very choosy and even ate any dead dinosaurs it could find.

SMARTEST DINOSAUR

If having a big brain makes you smart, then *Troodon* was the smartest dinosaur ever. For its size, it had the largest brain of any dinosaur. It was as smart as an ostrich, and smarter than any lizard or snake today. Along with that good-sized brain, *Troodon's* sharp eyesight and keen sense of smell made it a good hunter.

DUMBEST DINOSAUR

Diplodocus had the smallest brain of any dinosaur for its size, so you could say that it was the dumbest dinosaur. It was one of the longest dinosaurs ever and weighed more than four elephants, but its brain weighed only as much as a small melon.

Diplodocus had its nostrils in a weird place — they were on top of its head, almost between its eyes. This dinosaur's feet were specially built to keep it from slipping in the mud.

BEST PARENT

Maiasaura took good care of its young. The mother laid her eggs carefully in two layers, with sand around them to keep them warm. Then she mounded plants on top. As the plants rotted, they made heat and kept the eggs warm. When the eggs hatched, the parents brought food to the nest. These dinosaurs lived in huge herds. Many *Maiasaura* skeletons have broken tail bones. That makes scientists think these dinosaurs were very clumsy and often stepped on each other.

BIGGEST EGG

All dinosaurs laid eggs. The eggs that *Hypselosaurus* laid were about the size of a small watermelon, or big enough for a cat to curl up in. *Hypselosaurus* eggs have been found in pairs in straight lines, as if they had been laid while the mother dinosaur was walking. Scientists think that she did this to keep from stepping or sitting on her own eggs and squashing them.

MOST POPULAR

This dinosaur used to be known as *Brontosaurus*, but today scientists call it *Apatosaurus*. It's probably the most popular and famous dinosaur because its skeleton was one of the first really large ones found. *Apatosaurus* was a plant eater and was always on the move searching for food. It probably travelled in family groups, with the babies in the middle for protection. This dinosaur's body was longer than two school buses, and its tail was even longer. It may have used its tail as a whip to protect itself from enemies.

STRANGEST TAIL

When *Euoplocephalus* swung its powerful, club-shaped tail, other dinosaurs got out of the way. One swing and it could knock another dinosaur off its feet. *Euoplocephalus* was protected all over with thick bony plating — it even had bony eyelids. It needed all the protection it could get because it was very slow and awkward. This strong giant had a good sense of smell, but probably it also used its nose to make snorting calls to keep in touch with other *Euoplocephalus*.

STRANGEST NOSE

Scientists think *Edmontosaurus* had special flaps of skin on its snout. It could fill them with air to help make its roars loud and clear. That made it easier for *Edmontosaurus* to call and find its family or to warn of danger. Even though this dinosaur was a plant eater, it had more than 1000 teeth! Scientists digging up *Edmontosaurus* skeletons have found the pattern of its skin pressed into the rock around its bones, so we know it had skin like an elephant or a rhinoceros.

BIGGEST PTEROSAUR

Quetzalcoatlus wasn't a dinosaur. It is known as a pterosaur or "winged lizard" because it had wings and could fly. That's something no real dinosaur could do. But it lived around the same time and in the same places as dinosaurs. Like birds today, *Quetzalcoatlus* had hollow bones, and it's a good thing, because it was as big as a small airplane! It was probably a scavenger, like a vulture, and spent much of its time soaring high in the sky looking for its next meal.

FASTEST DINOSAUR

Gallimimus ran on its hind legs and was as fast as any racehorse. It used its speed to escape from other dinosaurs. *Gallimimus* had no teeth, but its beak-like jaws were so strong it could grind tough plants, break open eggs and eat small animals. Its hands weren't built for holding things, but it could use its claws to dig for food and to spear insects and fruit.

SLOWEST DINOSAUR

Stegosaurus was so slow because it was so-o-o-o heavy. Since it couldn't run from enemies, it had another way to stay safe. Because of its odd body shape, enemies had trouble deciding which end was the head and which was the tail. That let this heavyweight turn its back and whack them with the spikes on its tail. Scientists now think that *Stegosaurus* used the big, bony plates on its back not only for protection, but to help it keep cool when the weather was hot and warm when it was cold.

FIERCEST DINOSAUR

Other dinosaurs ran as fast as they could from *Deinonychus*. It wasn't big, but it was ferocious and had big jaws full of long teeth. This dinosaur held on to its dinner with its strong fingers and used the big claw on each of its back feet to rip apart its prey. And *Deinonychus* kept those claws razor sharp by lifting them off the ground when it walked. It hunted alone or with others in its pack to catch dinosaurs much bigger than itself.

THICKEST HEAD

No one knows for sure why *Pachycephalosaurus* needed a skull 9 inches (23 cm) thick. Maybe it was to protect its brain during head-butting contests with others in its group. Or if another dinosaur decided *Pachycephalosaurus* looked like a good meal, this thick-headed dinosaur might have butted its attacker. The bony spikes on its nose helped it look very fierce, but it was a plant eater. It even preferred soft plants!

BIGGEST HEAD CREST

Parasaurolophus had a tube about as long as a baseball bat on the top of its head. Scientists aren't sure how the tubes were used, but the dinosaurs may have bugled through them to make their calls louder. Experts also think the tube of each *Parasaurolophus* was a slightly different shape or shade to help them recognize each other.

LONGEST HORNS

The horns above the eyes of *Triceratops* were about 3.3 feet (l m.) long, or longer than an adult's arm. This dinosaur had a huge head, about one-third the size of its body. Scientists have uncovered one *Triceratops* skull as big as a small car. That's the biggest skull of a land animal ever found. *Triceratops* used their horns and frills mostly for protection. Some skulls and frills have been found with holes in them, which tells scientists that *Triceratops* also used their horns when fighting with each other. Their skulls were specially shaped to cushion their brains when they fought.

THE LAST DINOSAURS

Scientists still aren't sure why the dinosaurs all died. Some think the weather suddenly became very cold. Others think a meteorite bumped into Earth and stirred up a thick cloud of dust that blocked out the sun. With no sunlight, all the plants died, and so did the dinosaurs who needed them for food.

One thing scientists do know is that of the 300 different kinds of dinosaurs they've found, probably only about 12 were left at the end. One of these was *Nanotyrannus*. It was a meat eater, and its teeth had jagged edges to help it catch and eat its dinner.

Leptoceratops was another of the last dinosaurs. It was a plant eater and might have stretched up on its back legs to try and grasp any delicious leaves that were just out of reach.

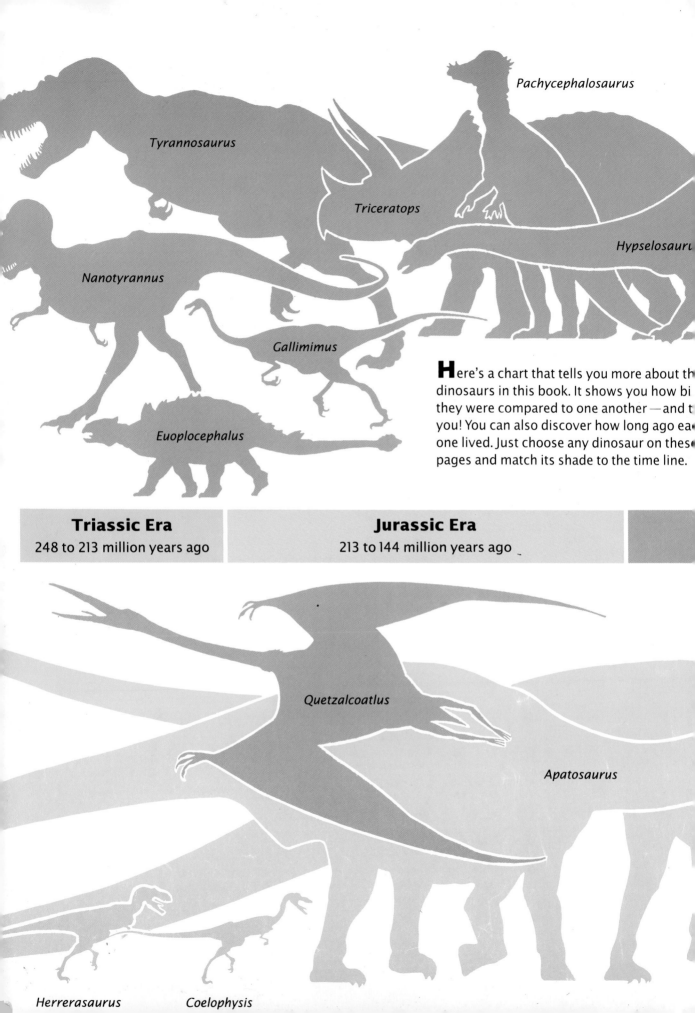

Pachycephalosaurus

Tyrannosaurus

Triceratops

Hypselosauru

Nanotyrannus

Gallimimus

Here's a chart that tells you more about th
dinosaurs in this book. It shows you how bi
they were compared to one another — and t
you! You can also discover how long ago ea
one lived. Just choose any dinosaur on these
pages and match its shade to the time line.

Euoplocephalus

| **Triassic Era**
248 to 213 million years ago | **Jurassic Era**
213 to 144 million years ago | |

Quetzalcoatlus

Apatosaurus

Herrerasaurus   Coelophysis

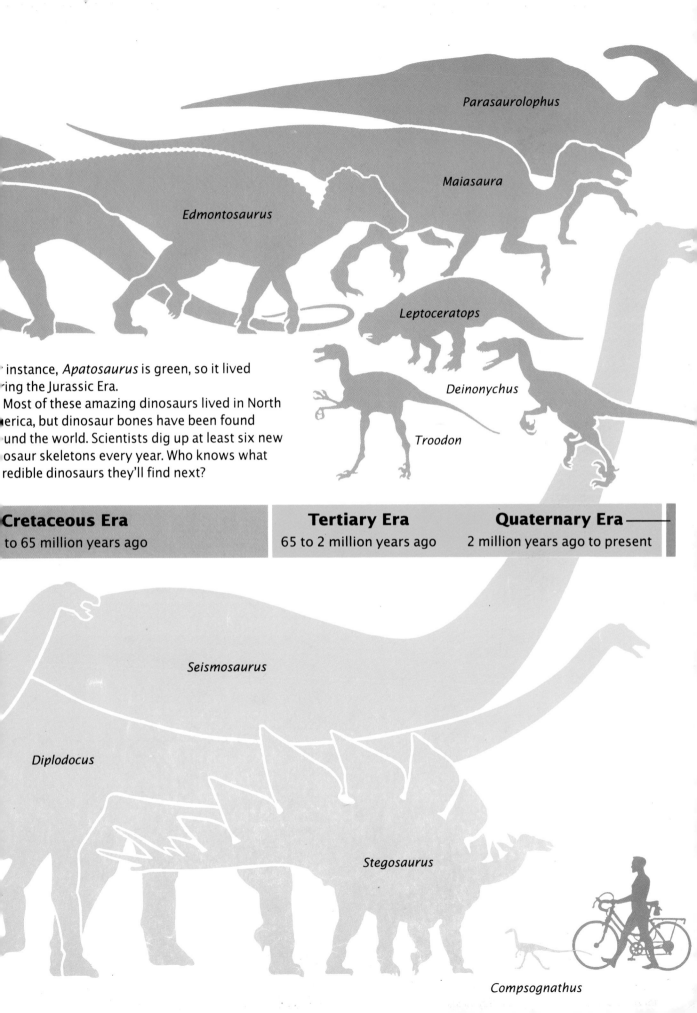

Parasaurolophus

Maiasaura

Edmontosaurus

Leptoceratops

Deinonychus

Troodon

instance, *Apatosaurus* is green, so it lived
ring the Jurassic Era.
Most of these amazing dinosaurs lived in North
erica, but dinosaur bones have been found
und the world. Scientists dig up at least six new
osaur skeletons every year. Who knows what
redible dinosaurs they'll find next?

Cretaceous Era	Tertiary Era	Quaternary Era
to 65 million years ago	65 to 2 million years ago	2 million years ago to present

Seismosaurus

Diplodocus

Stegosaurus

Compsognathus

With much love to Mom and Dad – E.M.

*To my wife Barbara, and my son, Daniel,
for all their love and support – G.S.*

*Many thanks to Dr Philip J. Currie, Head of Dinosaur Research,
Royal Tyrrell Museum of Palaeontology. He gave generously
of his time to make valuable suggestions on both the text and
illustrations.*

PUFFIN BOOKS
Published by the Penguin Group
Penguin Books USA Inc., 375 Hudson Street, New York, New York 10014, U.S.A.
Penguin Books Ltd, 27 Wrights Lane, London W8 5TZ, England
Penguin Books Australia Ltd, Ringwood, Victoria, Australia
Penguin Books Canada Ltd, 10 Alcorn Avenue, Toronto, Ontario, Canada M4V 3B2
Penguin Books (N.Z.) Ltd, 182-190 Wairau Road, Auckland 10, New Zealand
Penguin Books Ltd, Registered Offices: Harmondsworth, Middlesex, England

First published in Canada by Kids Can Press Ltd, 1994
First published in the United States of America by Viking,
a division of Penguin Books USA Inc., 1995
Published in Puffin Books, 1997

3 5 7 9 10 8 6 4

Text copyright © Elizabeth MacLeod, 1994
Illustrations copyright © Gordon Suavé, 1994
All rights reserved

Puffin Books ISBN 0-14-056162-5

The Library of Congress has cataloged the Viking edition under
catalog card number: 94-61733

Printed in U.S.A.